Sushi Simplicity

Making Mouth-Watering Sushi at Home

By Miyuki Matsuo

VERTICAL.

Foreword

Small and cute, simple and delicious.
These sushi will liven up the table with a pop of bright color.

Pair lovely yellow shredded omelet with lotus root cut to look like
a pretty flower. Combine pale pink *denbu* shredded fish with
salmon curled into a rose shape.

This is a collection of beautifully colorful, easy-to-make
homemade sushi that will please everyone from kids to adults.

The flavor profiles range from familiar favorites to
slightly unexpected combinations.

Try serving these during spring parties or at New Year's, for
home parties or potluck dinners, picnics, or boxed lunches for trips.

Please enjoy making these recipes on special occasions when you want
to serve something adorable.

Sushi Simplicity

Contents

Information for measurements, etc. used in this book

Measurements:
- In this book, 1 Tbsp = 15 ml, 1 tsp = 5 ml, 1 C = 250 ml
- All listed measurements for ingredients are approximations. Please make any adjustments you see fit depending on presentation style or condition of the ingredients.
- All sizes and volumes given are approximations. Please use them as guidelines open to change depending on presentation or arrangement.

Ingredients:
- Unless otherwise specified, sushi rice is prepared with rice vinegar.
- Ingredients labeled "boiled" are precooked. In the case of green vegetables, I recommend boiling in salted water to help preserve color.
- For pickles, be sure to thoroughly drain liquid before using.
- For Thin Fried Omelet, Shredded Omelet and Scrambled Eggs, let cool to room temperature before using.
- The *maccha* powdered green tea used in this book is meant for use in confections and is finer than the variety for making tea. It can be found in specialty shops.

Tools:
- After using plastic wrap to shape the sushi rice, remove and discard it.
- Use caution when handling cookie cutters or ring molds as some edges may be sharp.

Serving:
- Unless otherwise specified, all sushi can be served as-is. Use soy sauce or other condiments as desired.

Prep for Making Sushi at Home

Here's a simple round-up of
useful tools and basic preparations
that will help make at-home sushi attractive,
delicious and, above all, simple.

Basics ❶ Tools

People tend to think making sushi is difficult, but the recipes in this book can be prepared with just a few simple tools. Approach it with an easy-going attitude.

Making Sushi Rice

These are all you need to make delicious sushi rice. Choose the size and shape of the bowls based on the amount you'll need.

a Wooden Sushi Rice Bowl (*handai*)

Wood absorbs excess moisture from cooked rice, making the rice delicious. Rinse the inside of bowl and underside of the lid then wipe with a dry cloth before using.

b Bowl

Have several bowls at the ready for mixing ingredients and rice. Use smaller bowls when working with small portions of ingredients.

c Wooden Spoon

Use to stir vinegar into rice or to stuff rice into molds. As with the rice bowl, rinse lightly and wipe dry before use.

d Dishcloth, Hand Towel

Use when steaming rice. Pick a size that will cover the diameter of the rice bowl when there's rice inside.

e Fan

This is a necessary tool if you want delicious sushi rice. Fanning to cool the rice will give you glossy, non-sticky rice.

Making Shapes

Neat, showy presentations make cuisine all the more enjoyable. Use these tools to easily push your sushi up a notch.

a Cake Mold
Use to make larger sushi presentations.

b Ring Mold
Lacking a bottom, the ring mold is pulled out before serving.

c Bread, Confectionery Mold
Since these are flipped over to dislodge the sushi rice, use flexible silicone molds.

d Cookie Cutter
Use for pressed sushi or to cut decorative shapes out of vegetables.

e Plastic Wrap
Use to shape sushi into neat ball shapes, etc.

f Milk Carton
The inside of a milk carton is smooth, making it perfect for molding as sushi rice won't stick to it.

Use chopsticks and spoons for easy plating

Chopsticks and teaspoons can be handy for arranging food items too small for fingertips. They'll help you arrange tiny ingredients quickly and neatly.

Basics ❷ Preparing Sushi Rice

Once you get the hang of making sushi rice, it's surprisingly simple.
The refreshing fragrance of vinegar mixed with the subtly sweet rice enhances
the flavors of the toppings. Make as much or as little as you need.

Basic Sushi Rice

Ingredients
1 1/2 C white rice
1 1/2 C water
A
   3 Tbsp rice vinegar
   2 Tbsp sugar
   1 tsp salt
*Photos show 3 C of rice

Multigrain Rice

For multigrain rice, measure out
1 1/2 C white rice, remove 3 Tbsp,
and add 3 Tbsp of multigrain
mixture. Follow sushi rice directions
for cooking and seasoning.

Prep:

Rinse wooden bowl, lid and spoon
and wipe dry with a cloth.

01 Rinse rice and drain in strainer for 30
minutes.

02 Add rice and water to rice cooker
and cook normally. (If your cooker
has a setting for sushi rice, follow the
instructions and adjust amount of
water.)

03 Combine mixture A. Stir thoroughly
until dissolved.

04 Once rice is done cooking, transfer
immediately to bowl. Pour mixture A
evenly over rice.

05 Spread rice out to fill bowl.

06 While fanning rice, quickly stir with
wood spoon using chopping motions.

07 Cover with lid (or damp, well-wrung
cloth) to cool.

Basics ❸ Egg Prep

Here I'll show you how to make Thin Omelet, Shredded Omelet and Scrambled Eggs. The lovely yellow color is key. Make sure you follow the directions so you end up with pretty omelets that are never burnt.

Thin Omelet, Shredded Omelet

Ingredients (yields 2)
2 eggs
A
| 1 tsp sugar
| Dash salt
Vegetable oil, as needed

* Please use a teflon-coated frying pan.
* A 10" pan will yield 2 omelets; an 8" pan will yield 3. Photos show a 10" pan.

01 Crack eggs into a bowl. Add mixture A and whisk gently. Pour through a fine-mesh strainer, if available.

02 Heat frying pan over medium-low. Pour in oil and spread in a thin layer on pan with a paper towel. Pour in half of eggs, rock to spread across pan.

03 Once surface is dried, flip over and cook briefly. If it's dried out enough, it won't fall apart.

04 Drape omelet on an overturned strainer and let cool. Repeat with remaining egg mixture.

For Shredded Omelet, cut omelet in half, stack halves then julienne.

Scrambled Eggs

Ingredients
2 eggs
A
| 2 tsp sugar
| 2 tsp mirin
| Dash salt

01 Add eggs and mixture A to a pan and stir to combine.

02 Heat pan over medium and stir eggs with 4 cooking chopsticks. Stir constantly until eggs are thoroughly cooked and crumbly.

Basics ❹ Pickle Prep

The flavor and texture of pickles make them the perfect accent for sushi. Keep in mind how long they need to steep before use when making preparations.

Sesame Ponzu Pickled Burdock

Ingredients
1 burdock (salsify)
A
    5 Tbsp ponzu
    1 Tbsp ground white sesame seeds

01 Scrape off burdock skin with the back of a knife and cut into thin, long shavings. Soak in water for 10 minutes. Combine mixture A in a storage container.

02 Drain burdock, boil in water, drain again. While still hot, add to storage container and stir to coat with mixture A. Let steep for at least 20 minutes, stirring occasionally.

Flip over to allow seasoning to soak in evenly.

This recipe works with lotus roots, daikon, turnips and carrots, too.

Lemon Pickled Radish

Ingredients
5 radishes
A
    2 Tbsp lemon juice
    2 tsp honey
    Dash salt

01 Slice radishes into thin rounds.

02 Combine mixture A in a storage container. Add radishes. Let steep for at least 20 minutes.

The mellow sweetness of honey adds depth to the flavor.

This recipe works with ginger root, ginger sprouts, cucumbers, daikon, turnips and celery, too.

Sweet Pickled Lotus Root

Ingredients
3 1/2 oz lotus root
A
    1/2 C vinegar
    1/2 C water
    3 Tbsp sugar
    1/8 tsp salt

01 Peel lotus root and slice into 1/8" rounds. Make 1/8" triangular cuts on outer edge between holes to create flower shapes.

02 Boil lotus root in water with an extra dash of vinegar. Drain.

03 Combine mixture A in a storage container. Add still-hot lotus root. Let steep for at least 30 minutes.

Work on a cutting board for ease when cutting into decorative shapes.

This recipe works with ginger root, ginger sprouts and carrots, too. If using cucumbers, daikon, celery or radishes, rub with salt instead of boiling before pickling.

Part 1

Small and Sweet
Ball Sushi

Bite-sized round sushi are adorable
and neat but super simple to make.
Have fun combining all kinds of ingredients
to make them your own.

Octopus

Shredded Omelet & *Ikura*

Salmon

Tuna

* See p 25 for instructions

Broad Bean

Sweet Pickled Lotus Root

Smoked Salmon

* See p 26 for instructions

Scallop   Shrimp

Lemon Pickled Radish   Squid

* See pp 26-27 for instructions

Shrimp & Avocado

Italian-Style Octopus

Smoked Ham & Cream Cheese

* See p 27 for instructions

Pickled Red Radish

Salted Cherry Blossom

Red Kidney Beans

* See pp 27-28 for instructions

19

Squid Strips & Okra

Ham & Cheese

Omelet Wrap

* See p 28 for instructions

Mini Purse Sushi

Cucumber & *Tobiko*

* See p 28 for instructions

Mentaiko & Mayo

Scallion-Miso Grilled Tofu

Goya & *Ikura*

* See p 29 for instructions

* See p 29 for instructions

Basics of Ball Sushi

Cute, round little balls of sushi are enjoyable even just to look at. Plastic wrap lets you make them quickly and cleanly, and there are countless variations of toppings!

Instructions for Ball Sushi

Sizing of Ball Sushi

In this book, each Ball Sushi uses about 2 1/2 Tbsp (30 g) sushi rice. 1 1/2 C uncooked rice should yield 22 Ball Sushi. The measurements for sushi rice are only approximate. Adjust the size of each ball according to toppings or servings desired.

01 Place 2 1/2 Tbsp sushi rice on plastic wrap. Twist up ends of wrap tightly and roll rice into a round ball on your palm.

02 Place topping on a new piece of plastic wrap. Keep in mind how you want it to look as you arrange the ingredients. (Here, Shredded Omelet.)

03 Place ball of rice on top of topping.

04 Twist up ends of wrap tightly and roll ball on your palm, pressing topping into rice and shaping well to create Ball Sushi.

05 Remove wrap. Top with additional ingredients as needed. (Here, *ikura*.)

Note

Some ingredients are best added after.

For toppings that don't take well to wrapping (tough or soft foods or ingredients steeped in liquid, etc.), simply place on top of ball-shaped rice without using plastic wrap. Adjust according to the ingredients to keep them from falling apart.
*Photo shows Sweet Pickled Lotus Root.

To make: pp 14-15

Octopus

Ingredients (yields 1)
2 1/2 Tbsp sushi rice
1 slice sushi-grade octopus
Dash wasabi paste

Instructions
1 Form sushi rice into a ball using plastic wrap.
2 Place octopus on another piece of plastic wrap. Top with sushi rice, twist up wrap and shape into ball.
3 Top with a dab of wasabi.

Shredded Omelet & *Ikura*

Ingredients (yields 1)
2 1/2 Tbsp sushi rice
Shredded Omelet, as needed (p 11)
1 tsp *ikura* (salted salmon roe)

Instructions
1 Form sushi rice into a ball using plastic wrap.
2 Place omelet on another piece of plastic wrap. Top with sushi rice, twist up wrap and shape into ball.
3 Top with *ikura*.

Salmon

Ingredients (yields 1)
2 1/2 Tbsp sushi rice
1 slice sushi-grade salmon

Instructions
1 Form sushi rice into a ball using plastic wrap.
2 Place salmon on another piece of plastic wrap. Top with sushi rice, twist up wrap and shape into ball.

Tuna

Ingredients (yields 1)
2 1/2 Tbsp sushi rice
1 slice sushi-grade tuna

Instructions
1 Form sushi rice into a ball using plastic wrap.
2 Place tuna on another piece of plastic wrap. Top with sushi rice, twist up wrap and shape into ball.

Broad Bean

Ingredients (yields 1)

A
| 2 1/2 Tbsp sushi rice
| 1/2 tsp *mentaiko* (spicy cod roe)
1 boiled broad bean

Instructions

1 Combine A and form into a ball using plastic wrap.
2 Place bean on another piece of plastic wrap. Top with sushi rice, twist up wrap and shape into ball.

Sweet Pickled Lotus Root

Ingredients (yields 1)
2 1/2 Tbsp multigrain sushi rice (p 10)
1 piece Sweet Pickled Lotus Root (p 12)
Sprig daikon sprout

Instructions

1 Form rice into a ball using plastic wrap.
2 Top rice ball with lotus root and daikon sprout.

Smoked Salmon

Ingredients (yields 1)
2 1/2 Tbsp sushi rice
Few slices onion
1/2 slice smoked salmon
Sprig fresh dill
Dash coarse-ground black pepper
Slice lemon

Instructions

1 Thinly slice onion and soak in water for 10 minutes. Drain.
2 Form sushi rice into a ball using plastic wrap.
3 Place smoked salmon on another piece of plastic wrap. Top with sushi rice, twist up wrap and shape into ball.
4 Top sushi with onions, dill and pepper. Serve with lemon and squeeze onto sushi before consuming.

Scallop

Ingredients (yields 1)
2 1/2 Tbsp sushi rice
1 sushi-grade scallop, halved widthwise
2 tips scallion

Instructions

1 Form sushi rice into a ball using plastic wrap.
2 Place 1 slice scallop on another piece of plastic wrap. Top with sushi rice, twist up wrap and shape into ball.
3 Top with scallion tips.

Lemon Pickled Radish

Ingredients (yields 1)
2 1/2 Tbsp sushi rice
3 Lemon Pickled Radishes (p 12)
Dash *yuzu kosho* (citrus pepper paste)

Instructions

1 Form sushi rice into a ball using plastic wrap.
2 Place radishes on another piece of plastic wrap. Top with sushi rice, twist up wrap and shape into ball.
3 Top with a dab of *yuzu kosho*.

Shrimp

Ingredients (yields 1)
2 1/2 Tbsp sushi rice
1 boiled shrimp
Sprig *mitsuba* (or watercress)

Instructions

1 Halve shrimp widthwise.
2 Form sushi rice into a ball using plastic wrap.
3 Place 1 slice shrimp on another piece of plastic wrap. Top with sushi rice, twist up wrap and shape into ball.
4 Top with *mitsuba*.

Squid

Ingredients (yields 1)
2 1/2 Tbsp sushi rice
1 slice sushi-grade squid
Pepper leaf (*kinome*) (or mint)

Instructions
1. Form sushi rice into a ball using plastic wrap.
2. Place squid and pepper leaf on another piece of plastic wrap. Top with sushi rice, twist up wrap and shape into ball.

Shrimp & Avocado

Ingredients (yields 1)
2 1/2 Tbsp sushi rice
1 small slice avocado
Dash lemon juice
1/2 boiled shrimp (halved widthwise)
Dash mayonnaise

Instructions
1. Drizzle lemon juice onto avocado.
2. Form sushi rice into a ball using plastic wrap.
3. Place shrimp and avocado on another piece of plastic wrap. Top with sushi rice, twist up wrap and shape into ball.
4. Drizzle with mayonnaise.

Italian-Style Octopus

Ingredients (yields 1)
2 1/2 Tbsp sushi rice
1 slice sushi-grade octopus
1 slice cherry tomato
Dash basil paste

Instructions
1. Form sushi rice into a ball using plastic wrap.
2. Place octopus on another piece of plastic wrap. Top with sushi rice, twist up wrap and shape into ball.
3. Top with sliced tomato and a dab of basil paste.

Smoked Ham & Cream Cheese

Ingredients (yields 1)
2 1/2 Tbsp sushi rice
1 small slice smoked ham
1 tsp (5 g) cream cheese
1 slice black olive
Dash pink peppercorns

Instructions
1. Form sushi rice into a ball using plastic wrap.
2. Fold ham in half and place on another piece of plastic wrap. Top with sushi rice, twist up wrap and shape into ball.
3. Soften cream cheese and place on sushi. Top with olive and pink peppercorns.

Pickled Red Radish

Ingredients (yields 1)
2 1/2 Tbsp sushi rice
Pickled red radish (store-bought)

Instructions
1. Thinly slice radishes and cut into desired shape with cookie cutters.
2. Form sushi rice into a ball using plastic wrap.
3. Place radish on another piece of plastic wrap. Top with sushi rice, twist up wrap and shape into ball.

Salted Cherry Blossom

Ingredients (yields 1)
A
  2 1/2 Tbsp sushi rice
  Pinch *maccha* green tea powder
1 salted cherry blossom

Instructions
1. Rinse cherry blossom, soak in water for 10 minutes to remove salt. Pat dry.
2. Combine A and form into a ball using plastic wrap.
3. Place cherry blossom on another piece of plastic wrap. Top with sushi rice, twist up wrap and shape into ball.

Red Kidney Beans

Ingredients (yields 1)

A
| 2 1/2 Tbsp sushi rice
| 1/2 tsp plum paste (*neri ume*)
2 boiled red kidney beans

Instructions

1 Slice beans in half.
2 Combine A and form into a ball using plastic wrap.
3 Top rice ball with beans.

Squid Strips & Okra

Ingredients (yields 1)

A
| 2 1/2 Tbsp sushi rice
| 1/2 tsp plum paste (*neri ume*)
1 slice sushi-grade squid
1 slice boiled okra

Instructions

1 Thinly slice squid.
2 Combine A and form into a ball using plastic wrap.
3 Top rice ball with squid slices in a flower pattern and place okra in center.

Ham & Cheese

Ingredients (yields 1)
2 1/2 Tbsp sushi rice
Sliced ham, as needed
Sliced cheese, as needed

Instructions

1 Cut ham and cheese into desired shapes using cookie cutters (or a straw).
2 Form sushi rice into a ball using plastic wrap.
3 Top rice ball with ham, then cheese.

Omelet Wrap

Ingredients (yields 1)

A
| 2 1/2 Tbsp sushi rice
| 1 tsp salmon flakes
Red bell pepper, as needed
Thin Omelet (p 11, fried in 8" pan)

Instructions

1 Cut bell pepper into desired shape using a cookie cutter. Slice omelet into 4 strips (you'll only use one.)
2 Combine A and form into a ball using plastic wrap.
3 Place ball on omelet strip and wrap. Plate so ends of omelet are underneath and top with bell pepper.

Mini Purse Sushi

Ingredients (yields 1)

A
| 2 1/2 Tbsp sushi rice
| 1 tsp canned tuna
1 Thin Omelet* (p 11, fried in 8" pan)
Boiled *mitsuba* (or chive)

Instructions

1 Combine A and form into a ball using plastic wrap.
2 Lay omelet inside a ramekin and place rice in center. Gather edges of omelet and tie up with boiled *mitsuba*.

*Add 1 tsp potato or corn starch to egg mixture to keep omelet from tearing.

Cucumber & *Tobiko*

Ingredients (yields 1)
2 1/2 Tbsp sushi rice
5 slices small cucumber
1/4 tsp *tobiko* (flying fish roe)

Instructions

1 Form sushi rice into a ball using plastic wrap.
2 Place cucumbers on another piece of plastic wrap. Top with rice, twist up wrap and shape into ball.
3 Top with *tobiko*.

Mentaiko & Mayo

Ingredients (yields 1)
2 1/2 Tbsp sushi rice
1 slice *mentaiko* (spicy cod roe)
Dash mayonnaise

Instructions
1 Form sushi rice into a ball using plastic wrap.
2 Top with *mentaiko* and drizzle with mayonnaise.

Goya & Ikura

Ingredients (yields 1)
2 1/2 Tbsp sushi rice
1 slice boiled goya (bitter melon)
2/3 tsp *ikura* (salted salmon roe)

Instructions
1 Form sushi rice into a ball using plastic wrap.
2 Place goya on another piece of plastic wrap. Top with rice, twist up wrap and shape into ball.
3 Top with *ikura*.

Scallion-Miso Grilled Tofu

Ingredients (yields 1)
2 1/2 Tbsp sushi rice
Fried tofu (*atsuage*), as needed
A
  1/4 tsp minced scallion
  1/4 tsp miso
  Dash sesame oil
Dash dried nori seaweed powder

Instructions
1 Slice tofu into 1/2" width, then into a bite-size piece. (You'll only use 1 piece.)
2 Combine mixture A in a small bowl. Baste onto tofu and broil for 3 to 5 minutes in a toaster oven.
3 Form sushi rice into a ball using plastic wrap.
4 Top rice ball with tofu. Dust with nori seaweed.

Yakiniku

Ingredients (yields 1)
2 1/2 Tbsp sushi rice
Vegetable oil, as needed
1 slice beef (rib, etc.)
Yakiniku (or BBQ) sauce, as needed
1/2 *shiso* (or mint) leaf
Mayonnaise, as needed

Instructions
1 Heat oil in a frying pan. Fry beef on both sides. Once cooked, blend with yakiniku sauce.
2 Form sushi rice into a ball using plastic wrap.
3 Place *shiso* on another piece of plastic wrap. Top with rice, twist up wrap and shape into ball.
4 Top rice ball with beef. Drizzle with mayonnaise.

Butter Soy Sauce Grilled Scallop

Ingredients (yields 1)
2 1/2 Tbsp sushi rice
Butter
1 scallop (halved widthwise)
Soy sauce, as needed
Dash minced scallions
Dash red pepper flakes

Instructions
1 Heat butter in a frying pan. Fry scallop on both sides. Once cooked, blend with soy sauce.
2 Form sushi rice into a ball using plastic wrap.
3 Top rice ball with scallop. Garnish with scallions and dust with red pepper flakes.

About rice, vinegar and seaweed

Sushi requires rice, vinegar and seaweed. All three ingredients are readily found in finer grocery stores, but here I'll discuss which are best suited for making sushi. Even among the same ingredients, there are different characteristics and flavor profiles.

White Rice, Multigrain Rice

For sushi, I recommend rice that's low on stickiness and has a mild flavor. Since sushi is consumed at room temperature, you'll want rice that's tasty even when cooled. Adding mixed grains to your rice as it cooks gives the sushi rice an added dimension of texture and color and makes it look like you put in a great deal of effort (even though it's very simple). If you add black rice, the purplish color will seep out into other grains, dyeing them an attractive, deep shade. The flavor and impression will vary depending on the blend of grains used, so try all kinds.

Vinegar

There is a wide variety of vinegars, from powerfully acidic grain-based versions to sweet and refreshing fruit-based ones, to black vinegar with its unique flavor profile. For the recipes in this book, I use rice vinegar, which boasts a mild flavor that pairs perfectly with all kinds of foods, including rice. It has a good balance of acidity and savoriness that brings out the flavors of ingredients it's used on. The flavor will vary depending on the manufacturer, so be sure to try all kinds to find what you like. Of course, you can also make sushi rice with other types of vinegar. Test out a range of vinegars and see what kinds work with which foods.

Seaweed

Use fresh, crispy, bluish-black nori seaweed. The smooth and glossy face is the obverse side, and the slightly rough side the reverse. Wrap around sushi with the glossy-side out for a pretty presentation. Korean seaweed (on the left) has a fuller flavor that's perfect for sushi recipes that involve kimchi. These recipes use large sheets (both Japanese and Korean versions are around 8.25 x 7.5"). Divide these sheets into sixths for just the right width in creating *gunkan*-style sushi.

Part 2

Stylishly Dished-Up
Cup Sushi

Line up these pretty,
colorful sushi in small glass dishes and
they'll look like candy on display.
These are perfect for potlucks!

Shrimp & Lotus Root

Smoked Salmon Flowers

* See p 35 for instructions

Basics of Cup Sushi

Since you simply layer the ingredients in a serving dish, there's no need to spend time shaping ingredients by hand or with molds. Make it look showy from the sides as well.

Using cups

Tightly pack sushi rice and fillings into the cups, but you don't need to press as hard as you would for pressed sushi. The trick is to keep the layers neat and even so they look great from the sides.

01 Pack sushi rice into the cup, filling in any gaps. Use a small spoon to even out the surface.

02 Layer fillings and more rice on top. Smooth out rice, then finish with more fillings.
* Here, Shredded Omelet.

Using food

Instead of cups, fill plum tomatoes or hard-boiled eggs with rice. Be gentle when handling the "cup" food so they don't come apart. Wipe off any excess moisture from the ingredients before using.

01 Slice off the top of a plum or cherry tomato and scoop out the pulp with a small spoon. Use a paper towel to soak up excess moisture.

02 Make small balls of sushi rice, adjusting volume to fit inside tomatoes. Place rice inside tomato, taking care to avoid tearing tomato.

Note

Try using all kinds of serving dishes

Use whatever dishes you like for cup sushi. Clear glasses and cups are best if you want to show off the neat layers of ingredients inside. Ceramic dishes give off a warm vibe. I recommend smaller dishes, keeping in mind the balance of ingredients and amount per serving.

Plastic Cups

Light and durable, plastic cups tend to have a wide opening that makes stuffing them with ingredients that much easier. Try using recycled veggie or candy containers, too. These are ideal for gifting situations.

Shrimp & Lotus Root

Ingredients (yields one 6.5 oz container)
1/4 C sushi rice
1/4 C multigrain sushi rice (p 10)
2 Sweet Pickled Lotus Roots (p 12)
2 slices (rounds) cucumber
2 boiled shrimp
1 pepper leaf (*kinome*) (or mint)

Instructions
1. Pack sushi rice into container. Smooth out surface.
2. Layer multigrain rice on top. Smooth out surface.
3. Top with lotus root, cucumber, shrimp and pepper leaf.

Smoke Salmon Flowers

Ingredients (yields one 6.5 oz container)
Light 1/2 C sushi rice
1 boiled snow pea
2 slices smoked salmon
2 tsp salmon flakes
Shredded Omelet (p 11), as needed

Instructions
1. Halve snow pea and cut out triangles in ends. Roll up smoked salmon into flower shapes.
2. Pack half of sushi rice into container and smooth out surface. Layer salmon flakes. Top with remaining sushi rice, smoothing out the surface each time.
3. Top with Shredded Omelet, smoked salmon and snow pea.

Serving sushi in glasses normally used for drinks lets you see both the glass and sushi in a whole new way. Stemmed glasses give an extra bit of brilliance that's perfect for parties.

Smoked Ham Salad

Ingredients (yields one 4 oz glass)
1/3 C sushi rice
1/2 plum tomato
2 small slices smoked ham
1/3 oz baby lettuce
1/4 tsp olive oil
Dash each salt, coarse-ground black pepper

Instructions
1. Remove stem from tomato and chop into small pieces. Fold ham lengthwise and roll up into flower shapes.
2. Pack sushi rice into glass. Smooth out surface.
3. Top with baby lettuce, ham and tomato. Drizzle with olive oil and dust with salt and pepper.

Edamame & Pickles

Ingredients (yields one 5.5 oz glass)
A
  1/2 C sushi rice
  15 boiled edamame (shelled)
1/3 oz *mizuna* (or arugula)
1 *takuan* (pickled daikon)
1 pickled red radish

Instructions
1. Chop *mizuna* into 1" pieces. Dice *takuan* and radish into 1/2" cubes.
2. Combine A and pack into glass. Smooth out surface.
3. Top with *mizuna*, *takuan* and radishes.

Here I used some foods' natural shape to best advantage.
The fun fact that you can eat the cup as well as the filling is a hit
with kids and adults alike.
Try turning your favorite foods into cups, too.

Hardboiled Egg

Ingredients (yields 2)

A
| 3 1/2 Tbsp sushi rice
| 1/4 tsp mayonnaise
1 hardboiled egg
1 slice boiled okra
Dash *ikura* (salted salmon roe)

Instructions

1. Halve egg and remove yolk. Slice off a small part of the bottoms of each egg half to stabilize.
2. Combine 1/2 tsp yolk and mixture A. Halve and roll into balls using plastic wrap.
3. Stuff egg whites with rice. Top one with okra and the other with *ikura*.

Cherry Tomato

Ingredients (yields 2)

A
| 2 1/2 tsp sushi rice
| Dash red *shiso* rice seasoning
B
| 2 1/2 tsp sushi rice
| Dash plum paste (*neri ume*)
1 red cherry tomato
1 yellow cherry tomato
Sprig daikon sprout
Minced scallion

Instructions

1. Slice off tops of tomatoes and scoop out pulp with a small spoon. Use a paper towel to soak up excess moisture.
2. Combine mixtures A and B separately and roll into balls using plastic wrap.
3. Stuff red tomato with A and yellow tomato with B.
4. Top red tomato with daikon sprout and yellow tomato with minced scallion.

For sushi recipes featuring meat, glass bowls show off the volume of the ingredients in a settled, subdued way. Ceramic and china bowls give a warmer impression.

Yuzu Kosho Chicken & Burdock

Ingredients (yields one 6 oz bowl)

A

> Light 1/2 C sushi rice
> 1/2 oz Sesame Ponzu Pickled Burdock (p 12)

1/2 chicken breast
1/6 tsp *yuzu kosho* (citrus pepper paste)
1/3 oz *mizuna* (or arugula)
1/2 radish
Dash roasted white sesame seeds

Instructions

1 Boil chicken breast. Once cooled, shred by hand and combine with *yuzu kosho*.
2 Chop *mizuna* into 1" pieces. Slice radish into thin rounds.
3 Combine A, pack into bowl and smooth out surface.
4 Top with *mizuna*, chicken and radishes. Garnish with sesame seeds.

Teriyaki Chicken Chirashi

Ingredients (yields one 5 oz bowl)

1/2 C sushi rice
1 oz chicken (thigh, boneless)
Dash salt
Dash vegetable oil

A

> 1/2 tsp soy sauce
> 1/2 tsp mirin
> 1 tsp water

Boiled carrot, sliced, as needed
1 boiled snap pea
Shredded Omelet (p 11), as needed

Instructions

1 Chop chicken into small pieces and dust with salt. Heat vegetable oil in a frying pan and fry chicken. Once thoroughly cooked, add mixture A and blend.
2 Cut carrots into desired shape with a cookie cutter. Open snap pea into halves.
3 Pack rice into bowl. Smooth out surface.
4 Top with Shredded Omelet, chicken, carrot and pea.

Using colorful ingredients, cleverly

A key point in displaying decorative sushi elegantly is the use of colors. Here I'll introduce some ingredients that I employ in these recipes to add a splash of color. They're also perfectly suited to sushi flavor-wise. They'll make your sushi satisfying both to the eye and the palate. Pay attention to the cute shapes, too.

Red/Pink Ingredients

a Pickled red radish

b Spicy cod roe (*mentaiko*)

c Red cherry tomatoes

d Boiled red kidney beans

e Red bell pepper

f Smoked ham

g Plum paste (*neri ume*)

h Shredded fish (*denbu*)

i Lemon Pickled Radish (p 12)

Yellow/Orange Ingredients

a Flying fish roe (*tobiko*)

b Corn kernels

c Smoked salmon

d Shredded Omelet (p 11)

e Salmon flakes

f Yellow bell pepper

g Yellow cherry tomato

h Pickled daikon (*takuan*)

i Salted salmon roe (*ikura*)

Green Ingredients

a Broad beans, edamame

b Pepper leaves

c Okra

d *Maccha* green tea powder

e Cucumbers

f Basil paste

g Snow peas

h Parsley

i Snap peas

Part 3

A Variety of Shapes and Styles
Simple Pressed Sushi

Use items you already have for easy-to-make pressed sushi.
Simply shaped molds are better than complicated ones,
as the sushi will retain the shape better once it's out of the mold.

Crab & Corn

Scrambled Egg & *Ikura*

* See p 47 for instructions

Basics of Simple Pressed Sushi

Pressed sushi looks complicated, but it's very easy if you use small molds.
The same ingredients can give a totally different impression based on the mold,
so try making pressed sushi in a variety of shapes.

Use molds that won't stick to the sushi rice

Since the rice is pressed into the molds, it can be easy for the rice to
stick. Be sure to use materials that will pull away easily, allowing the rice
to retain the shape of the mold. I recommend teflon-coated metal or
silicone molds, as they are easy to remove.

With all molds, rinse first to
prevent rice from sticking.

Using pudding cups

01 Place sushi rice in cup. Press and
smooth out surface using plastic wrap.

02 Add fillings and more rice. Smooth out
surface.

03 Flip onto plate and gently remove cup.

Using milk cartons and ring molds

Place mold on plate. Add rice. Press and
smooth out surface using plastic wrap.
Gently remove mold.

Note

Make your own mold with a milk carton

Thoroughly wash, rinse and dry a milk
carton and cut out a 1.5"-wide section
and you've got an instant pressed sushi
mold. Be sure to cut straight so the
mold is stable. Use a variety of sizes of
cartons to create a range of molds.

To make: pp 44-45

Milk
Carton

Not only can you make these molds at any time, you can create different shapes of sushi just by adjusting the placement of the mold. Use different sizes or change the height to create variations.

Crab & Corn

Ingredients

(yields one 1.5"-high section of a
milk carton mold)
1/3 C multigrain sushi rice (p 10)
1/3 C sushi rice
2 Tbsp canned shredded crab meat
2 Tbsp corn kernels
Sprig *mitsuba* (or watercress)

Instructions

1 Rinse mold and set on plate in a square. Add multigrain sushi rice. Press firmly and smooth out surface with plastic wrap. Top with sushi rice, press and smooth out.
2 Top with crab and corn. Gently remove mold.
3 Garnish with *mitsuba*.

Scrambled Egg & *Ikura*

Ingredients

(yields one 1.5"-high section of a
milk carton mold)
A
  1/3 C sushi rice
  4 Lemon Pickled Radishes (p 12)
B
  1/3 C sushi rice
  1/4 tsp dried nori seaweed powder
2 boiled snow peas
1 Scrambled Egg (p 11)
2 tsp *ikura* (salted salmon roe)

Instructions

1 Mince Lemon Pickled Radishes. Julienne snow peas.
2 Combine A and B separately.
3 Rinse mold and set on plate in a diamond shape. Add B. Press firmly and smooth out surface with plastic wrap. Top with A, press and smooth out.
4 Top with Scrambled Egg. Gently remove mold.
5 Garnish with snow peas and *ikura*.

Simple pudding molds are MVPs that work with all kinds of sushi but come especially recommended for recipes where you want to show off layers. The sushi tends to hold its shape relatively well while the mold is being removed, making these ideal for beginners.

3-Color Rice & *Tobiko*

Ingredients
(yields one 2.5"-diameter, 2"-high
pudding cup mold)

A

| 2 heaping Tbsp sushi rice
| 1/4 tsp yolk from hardboiled egg

2 1/2 Tbsp sushi rice

2 3/4 Tbsp multigrain sushi rice (p 10)

1 Thin Omelet (p 11), as needed

1/2 tsp *tobiko* (flying fish roe)

Instructions
1 Cut omelet into desired shape using a cookie cutter.
2 Combine A.
3 Rinse mold. Add rice from step 2. Press firmly and smooth out surface with plastic wrap. Top with sushi rice then multigrain rice, pressing and smoothing each layer.
4 Flip onto plate and gently remove mold. Garnish with omelet and *tobiko*.

3-Color Rice & Crab

Ingredients
(yields one 2.5"-diameter, 2"-high
pudding cup mold)

A

| 2 heaping Tbsp sushi rice
| 1/4 tsp yolk from hardboiled egg

B

| 2 1/2 Tbsp sushi rice
| Pinch dried nori seaweed powder

C

| 3 Tbsp sushi rice
| 1/2 tsp plum paste (*neri ume*)

3 slices (rounds) cucumber

1/2 tsp canned shredded crab meat

Instructions
1 Combine A, B and C separately.
2 Rinse mold, add A, press firmly and smooth out surface with plastic wrap. Top with B and C, pressing and smoothing each layer.
3 Flip onto plate and gently remove mold. Garnish with cucumber and crab.

Ring molds have no base. This means you can place them directly on the plate and remove them easily without causing the sushi to crumble.
The contrast between the flat pressed sushi rice and the airy ingredients on top is very sophisticated.

Salmon & Avocado Salad

Ingredients
(yields one 3.25"-diameter, 1.5"-high
        ring mold)

1/2 C sushi rice
2 slices sushi-grade salmon
1 slice avocado
Dash lemon juice
A
   1/2 tsp olive oil
   1/4 tsp Balsamic vinegar
   1/4 tsp soy sauce
1/3 oz baby lettuce
3 slices black olive
Dash each salt, coarse-ground black pepper

Instructions
1 Dice avocado and salmon into 1/2"
   cubes. Drizzle avocado with lemon juice.
2 Combine A.
3 Rinse mold and place on plate. Add rice,
   press firmly and smooth out surface with
   plastic wrap.
4 Top with lettuce, avocado, salmon and
   olive. Remove mold.
5 Drizzle with mixture A. Dust with salt and
   pepper.

Seafood Salad

Ingredients
(yields one 3.25"-diameter, 1.5"-high
        ring mold)

1/2 C multigrain sushi rice (p 10)
2 slices sushi-grade tuna
1/3 oz *mizuna* (or arugula)
1 tsp *tobiko* (flying fish roe)
Dashi shoyu (soy sauce with bonito broth),
   as needed

Instructions
1 Dice tuna into 1/2" cubes. Chop *mizuna*
   into 1" pieces.
2 Rinse mold and place on plate. Add
   rice, press firmly and smooth out surface
   using plastic wrap.
3 Top with tuna, *mizuna* and *tobiko*.
   Remove mold.
4 Drizzle with *dashi shoyu* before serving.

This book uses them to cut ingredients into shapes, but larger sizes also work as molds for pressed sushi. Use the same shape for the pressed sushi rice as well as the toppings for a refined presentation.

Scrambled Egg & Quail Egg

Ingredients
(yields one 2"-diameter, 1"-high
                 cookie cutter mold)

A
| 1/4 C sushi rice
| 2 tsp Scrambled Egg (p 11)
1 slice boiled carrot
1 slice hardboiled quail egg

Instructions
1 Cut boiled carrot into desired shape using a cookie cutter.
2 Combine A.
3 Rinse mold, add mixture A, press firmly and smooth out surface using plastic wrap.
4 Remove sushi rice from mold. Top with carrot and quail egg.

Shibazuke & Plum Paste

Ingredients
(yields one 2"-diameter, 1"-high
                 cookie cutter mold)

A
| 1/4 C sushi rice
| 2 tsp *shibazuke* (pickled cucumber and eggplant)
1 slice daikon
Plum paste (*neri ume*), as needed
Sprig *mitsuba* (or watercress)

Instructions
1 Cut daikon into desired shape using a cookie cutter.
2 Mince *shibazuke*.
3 Combine A.
4 Rinse mold, add mixture A, press firmly and smooth out surface using plastic wrap.
5 Remove sushi rice from mold. Top with daikon, plum paste and *mitsuba*.

Brioche Molds

Using molds meant for baking brioche bread yielded lovely, 3-D sushi.
I added toppings to draw the eye towards the top,
making the most of the cone shape.

Denbu & Cherry Tomatoes

Ingredients
(yields one 3.25"-diameter, 1.25"-high
brioche mold)

A
| Light 1/2 C sushi rice
| 1 tsp *denbu* (shredded fish)
1 red cherry tomato
Shredded Omelet (p 11), as needed
Sprig daikon sprout

Instructions
1 Remove stem from tomato. Chop into wedges.
2 Combine A.
3 Rinse mold, add mixture A, press firmly and smooth out surface using plastic wrap.
4 Flip onto plate and remove mold. Top with Shredded Omelet, tomato and daikon sprout.

Shiso & Radish

Ingredients
(yields one 3.25"-diameter, 1.25"-high
brioche mold)

A
| Light 1/2 C multigrain sushi rice (p 10)
| 1 leaf *shiso* (or parsley)
5 Lemon Pickled Radishes (p 12)
1 pepper leaf (*kinome*) (or mint)

Instructions
1 Mince *shiso*.
2 Combine A.
3 Rinse mold, add mixture A, press firmly and smooth out surface using plastic wrap.
4 Flip onto plate and remove mold. Top with radishes and pepper leaf.

Silicone Molds

Silicone molds used for baking muffins, cupcakes, etc., come in a wide variety of adorable shapes and are easy to remove, making them ideal for pressed sushi. The smallish size is neat, too.

Mentaiko & Cheese

Ingredients
(yields one 2.5"-diameter, 1.25"-high pastry mold)

A
| 3 1/2 Tbsp sushi rice
| 1/2 tsp *mentaiko* (spicy cod roe)
Sliced cheese, as needed

Instructions
1 Cut out circles of cheese using a straw.
2 Combine A.
3 Rinse mold, add mixture A, press firmly and smooth out surface using plastic wrap.
4 Remove from mold. Place cheese circles in a heart shape on sushi.

Egg & Ham

Ingredients
(yields one 2.5"-diameter, 1.25"-high pastry mold)

A
| 3 1/2 Tbsp sushi rice
| 1/3 tsp yolk from hardboiled egg
Sliced roasted ham, as needed

Instructions
1 Cut out circles of ham using a straw.
2 Combine A.
3 Rinse mold, add mixture A, press firmly and smooth out surface using plastic wrap.
4 Remove from mold. Place ham circles in a heart shape on sushi.

Have fun with presentation

Small, cute sushi are especially fun to set out on the table.
The same sushi will look totally different depending on how they're plated.
Enjoy various stylings to match the occasion and your guests.

Space sushi evenly on a square plate

For an elegant presentation, place them at even intervals so they aren't too close together. Each individual piece gets equal attention, emphasizing the balance of the color palette. Recommended for girls' nights, parties with only adults or with your elders present.

Tightly pack together on a round plate

A bunch of cute sushi all gathered together gives a lively, boisterous impression. Keep similar colors apart to create visual balance and a sense of variation. Highlight the fun of choosing which to eat at a party with lots of people or where young kids will be present.

Individual small plates for sushi

Giving each piece of sushi its own plate heightens their sense of specialness. Small plates emphasize how adorable these sushi are and make their nice colors look even more attractive. When you don't want to make that many sushi or want to treat each of your guests to pressed sushi, small plates are convenient.

The tablecloth is important

The cloth underneath plays a role in how the sushi looks. Use colors that suit the season and shades that match the ingredients of the sushi. Fit the mood you want to create.

Part 4

Rearranged Standards
Simply Special *Gunkan-maki & Inari*

Put just a touch more effort into making
standby staples *gunkan-maki* (battleship sushi) and
inari (fried tofu sushi) to make them even more special.
Enjoy these *gunkan-maki* that are as small as ball sushi.

Mentaiko & Cream Cheese in Seaweed

Ikura in Cucumber

Bell Pepper in Smoked Ham

Basil & Olive in Smoked Salmon

* See p 68 for instructions

Tuna & Avocado in Seaweed

Ground *Natto* in Cucumber

Radish & Edamame in Celery

Squid Kimchi in Korean Seaweed

* See p 69 for instructions

Shredded Omelet & *Denbu*

Shrimp & Flower-Shaped Daikon

Sweet Pickled Lotus Root & Broad Beans

* See p 70 for instructions

Sweet Boiled Chestnuts & Kidney Beans

Shibazuke & Sesame Seeds

Sesame Ponzu Pickled Burdock & Edamame

* See p 71 for instructions

Scrambled Egg & Salmon

Mentaiko & Quail Egg

* See p 71 for instructions

Basics of Special *Gunkan-maki*

Simply wrap a ball of sushi rice with the traditional nori seaweed—or thinly-sliced vegetables for a special twist. The uniquely snappy texture of veggies is addictive.

Wrap with seaweed

A standard sheet of nori seaweed divided into sixths widthwise yields the perfect size for wrapping around 2 1/2 Tbsp sushi rice. The seaweed will be taller than the rice, which creates space to add toppings.

01 Place 2 1/2 Tbsp sushi rice on plastic wrap. Twist up ends of wrap tightly and roll rice into a round ball on your palm.

02 Divide seaweed sheet widthwise into sixths. Wrap a strip of seaweed around rice ball.

Wrap with vegetable

Thinly-sliced veggies are flexible because of their high water content and easily cling to sushi rice. Be sure the strip of vegetable is wide enough so it's higher than the rice ball when wrapped.

01 Use a peeler to thinly slice vegetable. Make 2 slices.

02 Wrap a strip around the lower portion of the rice ball.

03 Wrap second strip around the upper part of the rice ball.
  * Here, cucumber.

Note

Use strips that are wide enough

The first several strips of veggie you peel will be too narrow to use, so keep peeling until you get sections that are wide enough to make *gunkan-maki* (left pair in photo).

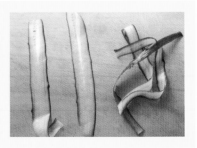

Basics of *Inari*

Sweet, salty and juicy, thin fried tofu make the taste. Try preparing them yourself. *Inari* might seem plain, but it can be very showy if wrapped right.

Sweet Boiled Tofu

Ingredients
5 sheets thin fried tofu (*aburaage*)

A

> 1 1/4 C *dashi* (bonito broth)
> 2 Tbsp each soy sauce, mirin, sugar

01 Place tofu on a cutting board. Gently roll a chopstick along the tofu to make it easier to open up.

02 Halve tofu widthwise and open into pouches, pulling apart with your thumbs.

03 Dredge through boiling water to wick away oil. (Or place tofu in a strainer and douse with boiling water.)

04 Add mixture A to a pot and stir. Add tofu and turn on heat.

05 Once boiling, drop a lid onto the tofu and simmer for 15 minutes, occasionally flipping tofu over in pot.

Note

Adding rice, folding the tofu

When you add toppings
Fold top edges of boiled tofu inside (see photo). Press rice into a football shape and place inside tofu pouch, keeping the edges intact. The folded section of tofu should be slightly higher than the rice.

When you want to seal rice inside
Press rice into a football shape and place inside boiled tofu pouch. Fold down left, right, front and back edges of tofu (see photo) and let settle.

To make: p 60

Mentaiko & Cream Cheese in Seaweed

Ingredients (yields 1)
2 1/2 Tbsp sushi rice
A
  2 tsp *mentaiko* (spicy cod roe)
  1/2" cube cream cheese (1 tsp)
1/6 sheet grilled nori seaweed
Fresh parsley, for garnish

Instructions
1 Combine A.
2 Roll rice into a ball using plastic wrap.
3 Wrap rice in seaweed. Top with A and garnish with parsley.

Ikura in Cucumber

Ingredients (yields 1)
2 1/2 Tbsp sushi rice
Cucumber, as needed
1 Tbsp *ikura* (salted salmon roe)

Instructions
1 Thinly slice cucumber into long strips with a peeler. Prep 2 strips.
2 Roll rice into a ball using plastic wrap.
3 Wrap 1 strip of cucumber around bottom half of rice ball. Wrap 2nd strip around top of rice ball, overlapping 1st strip.
4 Top with *ikura*.

Bell Pepper in Smoked Ham

Ingredients (yields 1)
2 1/2 Tbsp sushi rice
Yellow bell pepper, as needed
2 small slices smoked ham
Sprig fresh dill

Instructions
1 Cut bell pepper into desired shape with cookie cutter.
2 Roll rice into a ball using plastic wrap.
3 Fold ham in half lengthwise and wrap around rice ball. Top with bell pepper and dill.

Basil & Olive in Smoked Salmon

Ingredients (yields 1)
2 1/2 Tbsp sushi rice
1 slice smoked salmon
1 slice black olive
Fresh basil, for garnish

Instructions
1 Roll rice into a ball using plastic wrap.
2 Wrap salmon around rice ball. Top with olive and garnish with basil.

To make: p 61

Tuna & Avocado in Seaweed

Ingredients (yields 1)
2 1/2 Tbsp sushi rice
1 slice sushi-grade tuna
1 slice avocado
Dash lemon juice
1/6 sheet grilled nori seaweed

Instructions
1. Dice tuna and avocado into 1/2" cubes. Drizzle avocado with lemon juice.
2. Roll rice into a ball using plastic wrap.
3. Wrap seaweed around rice ball. Top with tuna and avocado.

Ground *Natto* in Cucumber

Ingredients (yields 1)
2 1/2 Tbsp sushi rice
Cucumber, as needed
1 Tbsp ground *natto* (fermented soybeans)
3 slices boiled okra

Instructions
1. Thinly slice cucumber into long strips with a peeler. Prep 2 strips.
2. Roll rice into a ball using plastic wrap.
3. Wrap 1 strip of cucumber around bottom half of rice ball. Wrap 2nd strip around top of rice ball, overlapping 1st strip.
4. Top with *natto* and okra.

Radish & Edamame in Celery

Ingredients (yields 1)
2 1/2 Tbsp multigrain sushi rice (p 10)
Celery, as needed
1 slice radish
1 boiled edamame (shelled)

Instructions
1. Thinly slice celery into 8" strips with a peeler. Prep 2 pieces.
2. Roll rice into a ball using plastic wrap.
3. Wrap 1 strip of celery around bottom half of rice ball. Wrap 2nd strip around top of rice ball, overlapping 1st strip.
4. Top with radish and edamame.

Squid Kimchi in Korean Seaweed

Ingredients (yields 1)
2 1/2 Tbsp sushi rice
1/2 slice sushi-grade squid
1/3 oz kimchi
1/6 sheet Korean seaweed
Dash minced scallion

Instructions
1. Dice squid and kimchi into 1/2" cubes and stir together.
2. Roll rice into a ball using plastic wrap.
3. Wrap seaweed around rice ball. Top with squid, kimchi and scallion.

To make: pp 62-63

Shredded Omelet & *Denbu*

Ingredients (yields 1)
1/4 C sushi rice
1 boiled snow pea
1 Sweet Boiled Tofu (p 67)
Shredded Omelet (p 11), as needed
1 tsp *denbu* (shredded fish)

Instructions
1. Halve snow pea on the bias.
2. Shape rice into a football.
3. Fold top edges of tofu pouch inwards. Keeping them intact, place rice inside.
4. Top with shredded omelet, *denbu* and snow peas.

Shrimp & Flower-Shaped Daikon

Ingredients (yields 1)
1/4 C sushi rice
1 Sweet Boiled Tofu (p 67)
2 slices daikon (1/5" thick)
1 slice carrot (1/5" thick)
1/2 leaf *shiso* (or mint)
1 boiled shrimp

Instructions
1. Cut daikon into flower shapes with cookie cutter. Cut out center with a straw.
2. Cut carrot into circles with a straw. Stuff into center of daikon flowers.
3. Shape rice into a football.
4. Fold top edges of tofu pouch inwards. Keeping them intact, place rice inside.
5. Top with *shiso*, shrimp and daikon-and-carrot flowers.

Sweet Pickled Lotus Root & Broad Beans

Ingredients (yields 1)
1/4 C sushi rice
1 Sweet Boiled Tofu (p 67)
2 tsp *tobiko* (flying fish roe)
2 boiled broad beans
1 Sweet Pickled Lotus Root (p 12)

Instructions
1. Shape rice into a football.
2. Fold top edges of tofu pouch inwards. Keeping them intact, place rice inside.
3. Top with *tobiko*, broad beans and Sweet Pickled Lotus Root.

Sweet Boiled Chestnuts & Kidney Beans

Ingredients (yields 1)

A
- 3 1/2 Tbsp sushi rice
- 1 sweet boiled chestnut
- 3 boiled red kidney beans

1 Sweet Boiled Tofu (p 67)

Instructions

1 Finely chop chestnut.
2 Combine A and shape into a football.
3 Place rice inside tofu pouch and fold closed.

Shibazuke & Sesame Seeds

Ingredients (yields 1)

A
- 3 1/2 Tbsp sushi rice
- 1 tsp *shibazuke* (pickled cucumber and eggplant)
- 1/8 tsp roasted white sesame seeds

1 Sweet Boiled Tofu (p 67)

Instructions

1 Finely chop *shibazuke*.
2 Combine A and shape into a football.
3 Place rice inside tofu pouch and fold closed.

Sesame Ponzu Pickled Burdock & Edamame

Ingredients (yields 1)

A
- 3 1/2 Tbsp sushi rice
- 1/3 oz Sesame Ponzu Pickled Burdock (p 12)
- 5 boiled edamame (shelled)

1 Sweet Boiled Tofu (p 67)

Instructions

1 Combine A and shape into a football.
2 Place rice inside tofu pouch and fold closed.

Scrambled Egg & Salmon

Ingredients (yields 1)

1/4 C sushi rice
1 Sweet Boiled Tofu (p 67)
2 tsp Scrambled Eggs (p 11)
2 tsp salmon flakes
1 pepper leaf (*kinome*) (or mint)

Instructions

1 Shape rice into a football.
2 Fold top edges of tofu pouch inwards. Keeping them intact, place rice inside.
3 Top with Scrambled Eggs, salmon flakes and pepper leaf.

Mentaiko & Quail Egg

Ingredients (yields 1)

1/4 C sushi rice
1/2 boiled snap pea
1 Sweet Boiled Tofu (p 67)
2 slices *mentaiko* (spicy cod roe)
1/2 hardboiled quail egg

Instructions

1 Open snap pea into halves.
2 Shape rice into a football.
3 Fold top edges of tofu pouch inwards. Keeping them intact, place rice inside.
4 Top with *mentaiko*, quail egg and snap pea.

Organized by Theme: Sushi Recipe Index

You usually choose which sushi to make based on the main ingredient, whether it's seafood, meat or vegetable, but it's also fun to think up a menu based on the accent flavors and your guests' likes and dislikes. I've organized the recipes into three themed categories to help inspire your menu creation.

Spicy sushi suited to adults

- Octopus (wasabi) — p.25
- Broad Bean (spicy cod roe) — p.26
- Lemon Pickled Radish (*yuzu kosho*) — p.26
- *Mentaiko* & Mayo (spicy cod roe) — p.29
- Butter Soy Sauce Grilled Scallop (red pepper flakes) — p.29
- *Yuzu Kosho* Chicken & Burdock (*yuzu kosho*) — p.41
- *Mentaiko* & Cream Cheese in Seaweed (spicy cod roe) — p.68
- Squid Kimchi in Korean Seaweed (kimchi) — p.69
- *Mentaiko* & Quail Egg (spicy cod roe) — p.71

Sushi using store-bought ingredients

- Sweet Pickled Lotus Root — p.26
- Lemon Pickled Radish — p.26
- Pickled Red Radish — p.27
- Shrimp & Lotus Root — p.35
- Edamame & Pickles — p.37
- *Yuzu Kosho* Chicken & Burdock — p.41
- Scrambled Egg & *Ikura* — p.47
- *Shibazuke* & Plum Paste — p.53
- *Shiso* & Radish — p.55
- Sweet Pickled Lotus Root & Broad Beans — p.70
- *Shibazuke* & Sesame Seeds — p.71
- Sesame Ponzu Pickled Burdock & Edamame — p.71

Sushi recommended for children

- Ham & Cheese — p.28
- Omelet Wrap — p.28
- Mini Purse Sushi — p.28
- Yakiniku — p.29
- Smoked Salmon Flowers — p.35
- Hardboiled Egg — p.39
- Cherry Tomato — p.39
- Teriyaki Chicken Chirashi — p.41
- Crab & Corn — p.47
- 3-Color Rice & *Tobiko* — p.49
- 3-Color Rice & Crab — p.49
- Scrambled Egg & Quail Egg — p.53
- Egg & Ham — p.57

Save for a Special Occasion!

Cake Sushi

Sushi shaped like a cake is the perfect item to
serve at a party filled with people you love.
Pretty decorations combined with a
voluminous serving size are a treat.
Your guests will definitely be thrilled.

Capitalize on the shape of ball sushi
by lining them up on a plate

Wreath Sushi

Even if you don't have a large mold, you can create a party-perfect presentation
with smaller sushi. Since each piece is shaped separately, this is easy to share.

Ingredients (yields 1 plate)

A
- 3/4 C + 1 Tbsp sushi rice
- 1 Tbsp *mentaiko* (spicy cod roe)

3/4 C + 1 Tbsp sushi rice
Sliced cheese, as needed
5 small slices smoked ham
5 slices red cherry tomato
Fresh dill, for garnish

Instructions

1 Cut cheese into desired shape with cookie
   cutter.
2 Combine A, divide into fifths and roll into balls
   using plastic wrap.
3 Roll sushi rice into balls using plastic wrap.
4 Fold ham in half, place on a separate piece of
   plastic wrap and top with sushi rice. Twist up
   plastic wrap and roll into a ball. Repeat with
   remaining ham.
5 Arrange alternating sushi balls in a wreath
   pattern on plate.
6 Top *mentaiko* rice balls with tomato slices
   and garnish with dill. Top ham rice balls with
   cheese.

Note

The color scheme changes up the image

Here I used two types of ball sushi, but adding more types or contrasting
colors will create a different mood. Sushi of similar colors all lined up
creates a grown-up impression, while contrasting colors feels like pop
art. Try making all kinds in a variety of color combinations. Having a
wide range of sushi available makes choosing which to eat all the more
enjoyable.

Transform standard ingredients into something stylish

Sheet Cake Sushi

This sharp, rectangular shape shows off the lovely layers of sushi rice.
While I used standard ingredients like shredded omelet and shrimp,
this presentation will appeal to a whole range of ages.

Ingredients
(yields one 3" x 8" pound cake pan)

A
| 1 2/3 C sushi rice
| 3/4 oz *denbu* (shredded fish)

B
| 1 2/3 C sushi rice
| 1/2 tsp *maccha* powdered green tea

2 boiled snap peas
2 eggs, prepared as
   Shredded Omelet (p 11)
4 boiled shrimp
4 tsp *ikura* (salted salmon roe)

Instructions
1. Open snap peas into halves.
2. Combine A and B separately.
3. Press A firmly into mold and smooth out surface with plastic wrap. Repeat with B.
4. Place plate on top of mold. Flip over and remove mold.
5. Top with Shredded Omelet, shrimp, *ikura* and snap peas.

Note

Just a little extra effort makes a better impression

You could just add the topping ingredients as they are, but opening up the snap peas makes them look more appealing. Taking the extra step of cutting vegetables with cookie cutters or creating decorative shapes creates a much more showy presentation. The most enjoyable part of making decorative sushi is being able to show off your own special brand of charm. Just add a little effort to make it really feel like a party.

Western ingredients + sushi rice = unexpected deliciousness!

Layer Cake Sushi

The refreshing acidity of sushi rice enhances the flavors of fresh tomatoes, cheese and avocado plus the savoriness of smoked salmon. With anchovies as the secret ingredient, this fresh new take on sushi will give your guests something to talk about.

Ingredients
(yields one 6"-diameter cake mold)
1 2/3 C sushi rice
1 avocado
Dash lemon juice
1/2 tomato
3 1/2 oz mozzarella cheese
A
| 1/3 oz anchovies
| 2 tsp olive oil
2 oz smoked salmon
2 leaves lettuce
Dash each salt, coarse-ground
   black pepper
Fresh basil, for garnish

Instructions
1 Slice avocado in half lengthwise, sliding knife around pit. Remove from skin. Cut avocado into 1/2" half-moons and drizzle with lemon juice. Remove stem from tomato and slice into 1/3" half-moons. Slice mozzarella into 1/3" half-moons.
2 Mince anchovies. Combine A.
3 Firmly press half of sushi rice into mold. Smooth out surface with plastic wrap.
4 Spread smoked salmon slices over rice. Repeat with avocado slices. Add remaining sushi rice. Press and smooth out surface with plastic wrap.
5 Place plate on top of mold. Flip over and remove mold.
6 Top with lettuce and alternating slices of tomato and mozzarella. Spread mixture A on top in a circle. Garnish with basil.

Note

Use all genres of cooking for inspiration for presentation and combinations

I used the frosting and fruits found on layer cakes as inspiration for decorating this sushi. Pay attention to the combinations of colors and the way ingredients are arranged. As with cakes, wipe off the knide blade between slices for a finer cross section.

Miyuki Matsuo

National Registered Dietitian, Food Scientist and Food Coordinator

After developing cafe and deli menus for a major food manufacturer, she became an independent food coordinator with a theme of balancing health and cuisine, working in the mediums of print, magazine articles, TV, the web and advertisements.

Photo © Shinichi Matsuoka

Staff

Design: Shoko Mikami (Vaa)
Photography: Masako Kakizaki
Styling: Yukari Takahashi
Editorial Support: Kanna Kubo

Sushi Simplicity
Making Mouth-Watering Sushi at Home

Translation: Maya Rosewood
Vetting: Maria Hostage
Production: Hiroko Mizuno
Grace Lu

OUCHI DE TSUKURERU KAWAII OSUSHI
Copyright © 2012 Miyuki Matsuo

Translation © 2013 by Vertical, Inc.
Published by Vertical, Inc., New York

Originally published in Japan by Kawade Shobo Shinsha Ltd. Publishers

ISBN: 978-1-939130-07-5

Manufactured in Singapore

First Edition

Vertical, Inc.
451 Park Avenue South, 7th Floor
New York, NY 10016
www.vertical-inc.com